LONDON'S NORTHERN HEIGHTS
Circular Walk

The **Northern Heights Circuit** is a **self guided trail**, nine miles long, taking in 350 points of interest around **Highgate, Hampstead and Hampstead Heath.**

Its **350 points of interest** – one every sixty yards - consist in equal number of historic buildings, associations with famous people, places or natural or scientific interest and illustrations of Britain's social history.

The circuit is divided into **five sections**. Each section starts and ends at a point easily reached by **public transport** and served by **pubs and cafés**. Though each section makes a good walk in its own right, sections can be **easily combined** to create a more challenging itinerary.

After a few days on the crowded tourist trail of central London the Circuit provides a refreshing opportunity to re-connect with **nature** and to explore those aspects of Britain's **heritage** which can't be found in the centre of so large a city.

The route and its documentation have been devised by **The Highgate Society** with the assistance of the Heath & Hampstead Society and the City of London's Hampstead Heath team.

The unique charm of Hampstead and Highgate Villages is that their streetscapes still mostly contain buildings from the 18th and early 19th centuries when they were **rural settlements**.

On Hampstead Heath, which connects them, **common grazing land** and **farmland** has miraculously survived relatively little changed since Medieval times. Its fringes offer superb examples of landscape architecture whilst its views over London have inspired some of England's most celebrated poets and painters.

The five richly illustrated guides to the Circuit all come **with detailed route maps**, instructions on how to follow the trail and a brief description of each point of interest.

A companion trail to the Northern Heights Circuit, the 15 mile long **Hampstead Heritage Trail**, takes in a further 500 points of interest along its 15 mile route linking **Camden Town** and **Alexandra Palace** via Hampstead and its Garden Suburb.

Golders Hill Park to Kenwood House

Golders Hill Park • *Hill House Pergola* • *Sandy Heath*
The Spaniards • *Kenwood House*

Planning your trip

The walk starts at the refreshment centre in Golders Hill Park and ends at Kenwood House. Allow two to hours for the 1.8 mile walk and further time to explore Kenwood House and Estate. Take care in winter to set off in good time since Golders Hill Park, the Pergola and Kenwood all shut in the late afternoon.

If you have already walked section four proceed directly to point 8 in this booklet.

The middle section of the walk, where it crosses Hampstead Heath, can be muddy after rain. Stout shoes are recommended. There are a couple of sections which may require reference to the maps in this booklet. Dogs are prohibited on one short section which is easy to avoid.

This section of the Northern Heights Circuit will delight people with an interest in landscape gardening since it passes through three magnificent examples of gardens created by wealthy estate owners. It is spectacularly colourful in May and late October.

For a longer walk you could continue using section one of the Northern Heights Circuit as far as Highgate Village. From there it is easy to return to your starting point at Golders Green Underground station or to continue to Archway Underground station using the 210 bus.

Although it would be equally enjoyable to walk this section in the reverse direction there are points on the route when finding your route would be less easy.

Children should find much to enjoy on this section of the Northern Heights Circuit.

Facilities

There is a café at the start of the walk in **Golders Hill Park**. Two thirds of the way along the walk you come to a historic inn, **The Spaniards**. At Kenwood you have the choice of two cafés, **The Brewhouse** and **The Steward's Room**.

There are public toilets at **Golders Hill Park Café**, at the **children's zoo** and at **Kenwood House**.

Reaching Golders Hill Park

Take the **Edgware** branch of the Northern Line as far as **Golders Green** Underground station. At the station exit head towards the big white building (El-Shaddai International Christian Centre, formerly the Golders Green Hippodrome) and walk round to the side facing the road (North End Road). Wait at the bus stop alongside the building for either the 210 (destination **Finsbury Park**) or a 268 bus (destination **Finchley Road**). Alight after three minutes at the second stop when the bus announces "**Hampstead Way**". Cross at the pedestrian crossing and you will find yourself at the entrance to **Golders Hill Park**. Bear slightly to the right. The **refreshment centre** is now straight in front of you. The walk from the underground station would take about twelve minutes.

Returning from Kenwood House

Just behind Kenwood House runs **Hampstead Lane**. Stay on the same side of the road to catch the 210 bus, destination Brent Cross, every seven minutes, via the entrance to **Golders Hill Park** to reach the **Edgware** branch of the Northern Line at **Golders Green**. Alternatively cross the road for a 210 bus, destination Finsbury Park Station, every seven minutes via **Highgate Village** to the **High Barnet** branch of the Northern Line at **Archway**.

Points of interest around Golders Hill Park and the Pergola

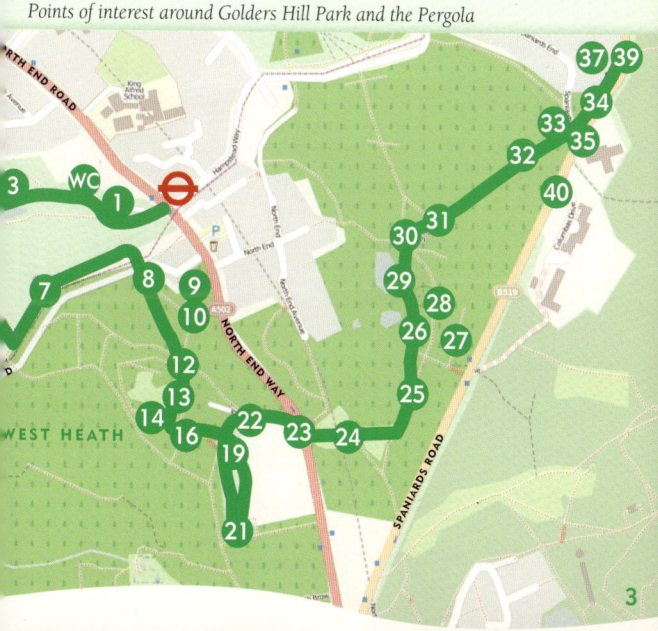

3

The Walk

1 This section starts at the café in **Golders Hill Park**. If you haven't already walked section four of the London's Northern Heights Circular Walk you would be well advised to begin this section with a tour of Golders Hill Park.

The park café

2 Golders Hill Park was originally the grounds of an 18th century **country mansion**, located on the site of the current park café and destroyed by enemy action in 1941. In 1898 on the death of its owner, Queen Victoria's surgeon, it was purchased for the nation. It is now maintained by the **City of London**.

Golders Hill House

Both Capability Brown and Humphry Repton are thought to have contributed to the park's design.

Whilst you are in the park dogs must be kept on leads.

The gardens and lake, Golders Hill Park

3 Walking downhill from the refreshment centre keep to the right and you will soon reach what was previously a kitchen garden. This now incorporates a walled **flower garden** and a pleasant **water garden**. Enter the garden and follow the path to the right of the pond and over a rustic stone bridge which crosses an **ornamental stream**.

Kookaburra at the children's zoo

Deer in Golders Hill Park

4 Bearing left along the contour of the hillside you will reach a recently renovated **children's zoo** and aviary. You can adopt animals here; a ring-tailed lemur for example costs £50.

5 Visible beyond the zoo is a children's **adventure playground** in a pleasant setting. There are toilets nearby.

6 Retracing your steps note an enclosure of **fallow deer**. Keeping this enclosure on your right walk up the hill towards an entrance gate.

The swings at the Adventure playground

7 Don't go through this gate. Instead bear left along a metalled path inside the park. On your left you will pass an early 20th century **bandstand** from which you get an excellent view across **Golders Green**, **Hendon** and **Mill Hill**. When you are opposite the refreshment centre turn right to leave the park through the entrance gate.

8 Cross Sandy Road, the track that runs parallel to the perimeter of the park, and climb a short flight of steps to a sandy knoll crowned with a small stand of **Scots pines**. Scots pines are not native to Hampstead Heath. Most were planted to enhance the landscape on knolls of thin, acid soils. The estate owners planted them to bring back memories of visits to Italy, fashionable at that time.

9 To your left you will see **North End**, originally a hamlet of humble cottages built by landless labourers on the edge of the Heath. The area of gorse bushes, known as the "drying ground",

Scots pines near North End

acquired its name from the practice of washerwomen using the bushes for drying clothes.

10 It was to North End that Charles Dickens had Bill Sikes flee from London and fall asleep under a hedge after killing Nancy in **Oliver Twist**.

11 When the **Northern Line** was extended from Hampstead to Golders Green in 1907 a station was to have been built at North End. The plan was abandoned once the farmland that it had been assumed would be sold for residential development was purchased to extend Hampstead Heath by what is now known as the "**Heath Extension**". The underground platforms were built and can still be seen from passing trains.

12 From the pines continue in the same general direction, circumnavigating the obstacle caused by fallen trees. You will arrive shortly at a gate on your right which marks the entrance to **Hill Garden**, the garden of The Hill, now demolished. Dogs are not allowed here.

Hill Garden is one of London's least known and least visited gardens due to its poor access by public transport and distance from a car park. You may be able to see recently re-introduced heather near the entrance.

Hill Garden from the pergola

13 Inside the garden, turn to the right and then bear left down the slope to an **ornamental pond**. Beside it is a recently restored pavilion which was built in the 1920's to serve a tennis court. Though the lawn drops steeply to the right, the view to the west is blocked by the growth of vegetation since the garden was originally created, because animals no longer graze on the Heath beyond.

14 The views that the garden once enjoyed can be seen more clearly if you climb two flights of stone steps to the top of the structure immediately in front of you. This is the **pergola** - the largest and most elaborate example of its kind in Britain.

A pergola is a landscape feature consisting of a horizontal trellis supported on posts that carry climbing plants and which can be used as a covered walk. Pergolas were popular in the late 19th century as places to take a stroll amid rambling climbing plants and the scent of roses. Viscount Leverhulme, the soap magnate, commissioned **Thomas Mawson** to design this particular one in 1906.

15 At the top of the pergola turn to the right where you will find a small belvedere with an orientation table designed to provide a viewpoint across the landscape that **John Constable** so fondly painted. This view stretched along the Thames valley past Harrow-on-the-Hill as far as **Windsor Castle**. When the tree tops were lower this scene would often be framed, as Constable's paintings were, by turbulent cloudscapes driven towards this viewpoint by the prevailing winds.

The Pergola, Hill Garden

16 Walking back along the pergola you can enjoy the variety of climbing plants that have been re-introduced since its **restoration** in 1994. You look out across the wilderness to the path through **West Heath** which features towards the end of section four.

17 Recently, **brown long-eared bats** have been discovered roosting by the pergola.

18 Shortly you cross a bridge which rises up and over a track deep below and see in front of you the grounds of **Inverforth House**.

Inverforth House

Inverforth House was built in its current form by William Lever (1851-1925), later **Viscount Leverhulme**, who founded what has since become Unilever.

19 When he owned the house from 1904 until his death in 1925 its grounds were separated from The Hill by a public right of way. Dissatisfied by the physical constraints of his original estate he sought not only to acquire the house and grounds of The Hill but also to **terminate public access** to the right of way that divided the properties.

1st Viscount Leverhulme

Persistently thwarted by London County Council he came upon the solution of constructing the pergola in front of his grounds and extending it via this **bridge** into the grounds of The House which he consequently bought.

The bridge joining Inverforth House and Hill Garden

20 The task of creating this pergola was both facilitated and financed by the timely extension of the Northern Line under Leverhulme's property in 1905 since it enabled him charge the contractors for the right to raise **tunnel spoil** through a shaft and onto his property where it was used as backfill to the pergola.

21 Continue to the end of the pergola. Then descend a spiral metal staircase to ground level where you can walk back through the kitchen garden below the pergola until you reach a **garden gate** to access the right of way which so vexed Viscount Leverhulme.

22 Turn right under the bridge which you recently crossed. In the wall on your left you will see examples of **mis-shapen bricks** used to project an air of informality.

Soon you reach **Inverforth Close** and then **North End Way**, higher up the hill from the entrance to Golders Hill Park.

23 At Inverforth House cross this busy road with care at the refuge facing the Corporation of London sign. Keep to the path to the immediate right of the Corporation of London sign and cross one open

Entrance to Sandy Heath from North End Way

patch of **grassland**, then another. Continue in the same general direction, bearing slightly left, until you come to more open undulating ground, lightly vegetated except for the occasional mature oak tree.

24 This area is managed using **coppice rotation** to create a mosaic of different vegetation heights. This provides a variety of nesting conditions and prevents woodland encroachment.

Pathway between gorse bushes

25 The large area of gorse that can be found here provides a good habitat for nesting birds such as **long tailed tits**. At the point where the path comes close to the gorse take a left fork up a gentle rise.

26 You will shortly see to your left the first of **four small ponds**. It is one of the best ponds on the Heath for frogs due to its well vegetated and shallow nature.

Sand digging on Sandy Heath, 1867

27 The undulating landscape is the result of the thick beds of sand that covered this, the highest section of Hampstead Heath. The **sand** was excavated during the second half of the 19th century for use in the mortar needed for laying bricks. During war time it was used to fill sand-bags. These excavations had reduced the landscape to one of total despoliation when this part of the Heath entered public ownership in 1889.

300 year oaks on Sandy Heath

28 Evidence of the depth of working may be seen by comparing the level of the land with that of the roadway, Spaniards Road, which you can at times see to your right. It is also evident in places where the bases of **ancient oaks** stand more than a metre above the surrounding land, their roots still clearly visible.

29 How ponds survive in such a sandy environment may seem strange since they are not fed by springs nor do they drain anywhere. The explanation is that the sandy Bagshot Beds contain deposits of iron which when soaked in water  *Iron pan ponds* oxidise and cause the sand to coalesce into an impermeable sandstone layer known as **iron pan**.

30 Though the discolouration caused by the iron gives the appearance of pollution these ponds support distinctive and thriving eco systems. They support a population of smooth **newts** and **rudd**. A **heron** can often be found fishing and as many as 40 **mandarin duck** have been known to overwinter.

A heron beside the third iron pan pond

31 Beyond the third and largest pond, where you find a bench in the memory of Barbara Myers, you come across Sandy Road, a continuation of the track you crossed as you left Golders Hill Park. Turn right onto this path.

32 Towards the end of this easy path, twenty yards from the path on the right hand side, and just before it crosses another smaller path diagonally, you may be able to spot two spectacular **coppiced beeches**, reminders of the time when this common land was used as a source of timber.

Coppicing is a method of woodland management used since Medieval times. It involves repeatedly cutting young tree stems down to near ground level so that new shoots emerge which after a number of years afford more productive harvesting than if the tree had been allowed to grow unhindered.

33 Amid a stand of **fir** trees is one much taller one, believed to be the last of a group planted in about 1745 by John Turner from seeds gathered near Ravenna in Italy. This group was drawn by **John Constable** in 1820.

Evidence of coppicing

34 You reach a main road and a cluster of old houses. The house immediately in front of you is **Heath End House**, from 1889 the home of **Canon Samuel Barnett** and his wife, the social reformer **Dame Henrietta Barnett** (1851-1936).

Plaque in memory of Dame Henrietta Barnett

35 A friend of Octavia Hill, Henrietta Barnett from 1903 led the campaign to extend the Heath northwards from Sandy Heath through the creation by acquisition of the **Heath Extension**.

In 1904 Henrietta Barnett appointed the architect and town planner Raymond Unwin to design the layout for the nearby Hampstead Garden Suburb. The innovatory principles of Unwin's design have had a major influence on the town planning profession ever since.

Beside the roadway is one of the few remaining examples of the troughs erected by the **Metropolitan Drinking Fountain and Cattle Trough Association**. This was formed in 1859 to improve sanitary arrangements and to foster animal welfare.

Cattle trough

It was supported both by Queen Victoria's husband, **Prince Albert**, and by the **Archbishop of Canterbury**. By 1885 over 50,000 horses were drinking daily from the Association's troughs in London.

37 Beyond Heath End House is **The Spaniards**, an ancient oak panelled inn and tavern, full of character. Built in 1585 as a tollgate inn on the Finchley boundary, it formed the entrance to the

Upstairs room at The Spaniards

Bishop of London's hunting park. An original **boundary stone** from 1755 can still be seen in the front garden.

38 The pub has a great literary heritage. It was frequented by Dickens and mentioned in his "**The Pickwick Papers**". A regular visitor was the painter **Joshua Reynolds**, some of whose work is displayed at Kenwood House. Its proximity to Leigh Hunt's home in the Vale of Health (see section four) made it a regular haunt of **Lord Byron** and **John Keats**.

The Spaniards and the toll house

39 Opposite The Spaniards is an old **toll house**. In 1961 it survived a proposal to demolish it to improve the flow of traffic. Restored in 1967 and again in 2011, it continues its search for a new role whilst still impeding the traffic. Both it and The Spaniards are listed buildings.

Evidence of deer near The Spaniards

40 To continue your walk to Kenwood House retrace your steps past the cattle trough, cross the road at the pedestrian crossing, turn right and, after 30 paces, turn left at a small gap in the fence marked by a sign. This entrance to the **Kenwood Estate** is named after a local historian **C W Ikin**. The house and grounds are maintained by **English Heritage**.

Points of interest, Kenwood Estate

41 Many fine mansions around the Heath, once they became too expensive to run as private houses, were converted for use as nursing homes. More recently they have then been sold to **private developers** for conversion to luxury flats. St Columba's, to your right, is one such mansion, Inverforth House, Athlone House, beyond Kenwood House, on section one are others.

42 With the grounds of these exclusive properties to your left and right descend the trail, turning more steeply to the left after a short distance. Soon you emerge from the woods into the **West Meadow**.

Head straight on through the trees when you see the meadow and join the main path, turning left towards Kenwood House.

This area forms the western quarter of the Kenwood grounds and includes a gravel cattle track.

Trees left to rot where they fall

43 Slightly to the left is a good viewpoint from which it is possible to see **Witanhurst** and the spire of **St Michael's Church** in Highgate (see section one).

44 Further down in the fenced off section, **sphagnum moss** grows in an acidic 'flush' where ground water, trapped by clay in the soil, creates spring lines. Given the rarity of sphagnum in this region the area is included within Hampstead Heath Site of Special Scientific Interest.

Springs where sphagnum mosses grow

45 Turning left along this track it is now an easy walk, the track curving with the contour. The former **dairy farm buildings** of Kenwood soon come into view up the hill to the left. Soon afterwards keep right where the broad path forks in two and continue contouring until you come to a gate which marks the boundary of the formal gardens of Kenwood House.

Dogs must be kept on leads from now on.

46 Shortly beyond the gate in a clearing immediately in front of you is the work "**Reclining Figure**" by the sculptor **Henry Moore**. This is one of a number of works in the grounds of Kenwood House, including "**Monolith Empyrean**" (Heavenly Stone) by **Barbara Hepworth** (1953), who lived in Hampstead, and "**Flamme**" by **Eugene Dodeigne** (1983).

Reclining Figure, by Henry Moore

47 From this point you enjoy an excellent view of the country estate of **William Murray**, a Lord Chief Justice who subsequently became the 1st Earl Mansfield. It was his nephew who commissioned the most celebrated landscape designer of the age, **Humphry Repton** (1752-1818), to re-design the park surrounding Kenwood House. Repton was also consulted over the design of the estate of what subsequently became Golders Hill Park.

48 The original early 17th century house was bought by Mansfield for £4,000 in 1754. The commission of its interior redesign was awarded to **Robert Adam**, (1728 – 1792), one of England's best known designers of country houses.

49 Mansfield has a major place in world history because, as the judge in the 1772 Somerset case, he ruled that slavery was incompatible with English law.

Kenwood House was also the home for 30 years of **Dido Elizabeth Belle** (1763 - 1804), the illegitimate daughter of Lord Mansfield's nephew, Sir John Lindsay, a British Navy Captain, and an enslaved woman who he met when in the West Indies.

Dido Elizabeth Belle with her cousin Elizabeth

50 Mansfield was part a local network of philanthropists committed to the abolition of the slave trade and the emancipation of slaves. **Samuel Hoare**, who lived in Heath House by Jack Straw's Castle, was another stalwart abolitionist.

The bill to outlaw trade in slaves was guided to royal assent by William Grenville whose home was on the other side of North End Road. Between 1824 and its abolition in 1833 the parliamentary campaign against slavery was led by Thomas Buxton, who lived in North End.

51 Returning to the main path leading to Kenwood House you cross a small stream and find yourself approaching a terrace bordered by limes. Turn to the left, making your way through winding paths bordered by **rhododendrons** and **azaleas** which, when they were first planted in Repton's time, would have been exotic imports from China. These thrive on Kenwood's acidic sandy soils and provide spectacular displays of blossom in early May.

The west garden in May

52 This formal garden is artfully laid out to provide a variety of vistas of the house and the park interrupted by **rustic arbours** and **ivy clad tunnels**. This style radically differs from the geometric designs characteristic of earlier English garden design and of 18th century gardens in continental Europe.

53 This air of natural informality is enhanced by the remains of **giant oaks** blown down during the great storm of 1987.

54 The gardens are sheltered and overlooked from the north by the ancient woodlands that run along the crest of the ridge. They are inhabited by **jackdaws**, a rarity so close to London, and **ring-necked parakeets**, popular pets that in this instance have escaped captivity.

55 Walking around and perhaps across the lawns then back to the terrace you may want to stop outside the **Orangery** to look across Repton's estate. A **fossil** oyster shell can be

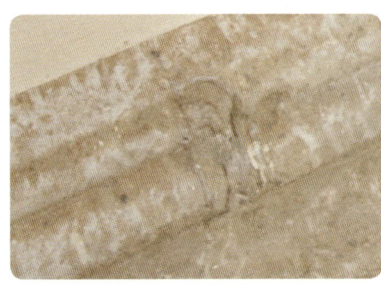
Fossilised oyster shell on a pillar outside the Orangery

seen at the foot of the left-most pillar of the Kenwood House Orangery. The Portland Limestone also contains shapes which are the burrows of creatures that once lived on the sea floor.

56 The little **white bridge** to the left of the lake is a single sided folly, but completes the view seen from the house perfectly even if Repton wanted to demolish it. When the estate was laid out it was possible to see ships in the Thames. Today it is difficult to credit you are standing in Europe's largest city.

Kenwood House, 1860

57 This terrace was the location for the wedding scene featuring **Hugh Grant** and **Julia Roberts** in the romantic comedy "**Notting Hill**" (1999). Summer concerts are held on the meadows below.

58 Before entering the house you can refresh yourself at **The Steward's Room** or **The Old Brewhouse** (disabled access, toilets). To do so continue along the terrace past a plaque commemorating the role of **Sir Arthur Crosfield** in the campaign to acquire Kenwood and its estate for the nation.

This campaign began in 1910 as a result of the introduction of **death duties** which had persuaded the 6th Earl of the need to sell the estate, he supposed for residential development.

Commemoration of Arthur Crosfield

This plan was shelved in 1914 but revived in 1920 and, as a result of Crosfield's campaign, Kenwood was secured for public enjoyment in 1928.

59 At the foot of the steps leading to the two cafés is a **bath house** from the early 18th century, a period when it was fashionable to take cold baths. It makes use of a natural chalybeate spring, the red colouration resulting from iron salts.

The bath room

60 Beyond the cafés is a **Ranger's Office** where you can learn more about the woodlands, wildlife and management of the Kenwood Estate.

The south façade of Kenwood House

61 To enter the house itself return to the terrace. Just beyond the **Orangery** at the opposite end of the terrace from the cafés, turn right through an **ivy clad tunnel** past ornamental gardens and right again to the main entrance of the house (entrance free, disabled access to ground floor, toilets).

Inside you can enjoy one of London's premier **collections of paintings**, including masterpieces by Rembrandt, Vermeer, Turner, Reynolds and Gainsborough, as well as the Suffolk collection of rare Elizabethan portraits. Make sure you also visit the library. The paintings were donated to the nation on the death in 1926 of **Lord Iveagh**, a member of the Irish family that owned the Guinness brewery.

Rembrandt: Self portrait

Brochures describing the House and the Estate and souvenirs can be bought at the gift shop.

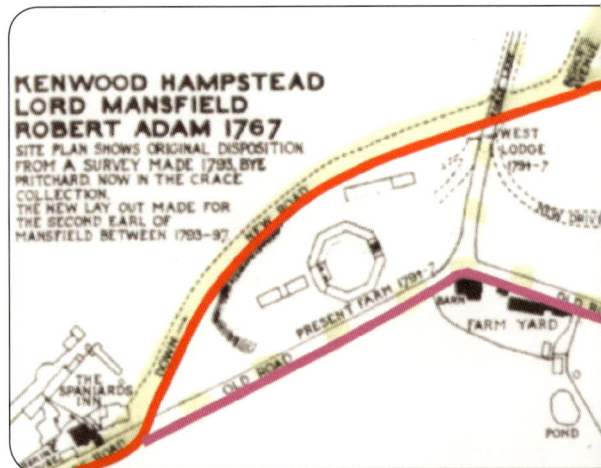

Diversion of Hampstead Lane to avoid Kenwood

62 Kenwood House marks the end of section five of the Northern Heights Circuit. You then have three choices: to follow section one of the Northern Heights Circuit which continues along the Hampstead-Highgate ridge as far **Highgate Village**; to follow the driveway from the main entrance back to **Hampstead Lane** and take a 210 bus (every eight minutes) from the same side of the road back to **Golders Green** Underground station; or to cross the road and continue to **Highgate** or to **Archway Underground** station using the 210 bus in the opposite direction.

63 Whilst waiting for the bus you may find it interesting to learn that Kenwood House used to be closer to Hampstead Lane, until the Earl of Mansfield found its proximity uncongenial and had the road **moved** from the purple to the red route in the map above. To screen his property he then planted the thicket of trees and shrubs you have just walked through.

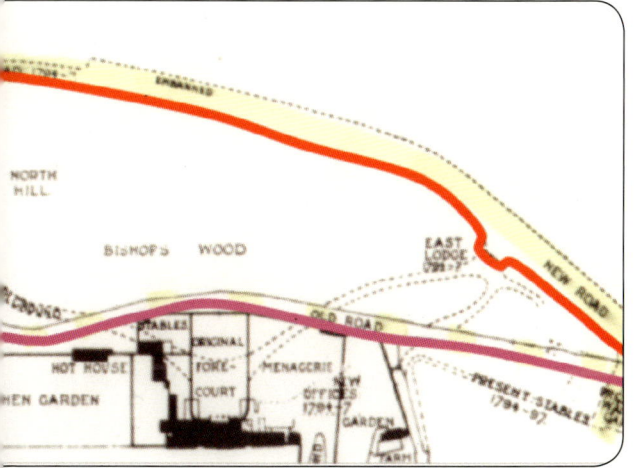

Further information

At **www.northernheights.eu** you can order the other booklets in this series, join the Society and provide feedback.

More detailed information about Hampstead and Highgate can be found in:

Denford, Stephen, The Hampstead Book
– The A-Z of its History and People, 2009

English Heritage, The Iveagh Bequest

Farmer, Alan, Hampstead Heath, 1984

McDowall, David, and Wolton, Deborah,
The Walkers Guide to Hampstead Heath, 2006

Richardson, John, Highgate: Its history since the 15th century, 1983

Schwitzer, Joan, Highgate Walks, 2004

© 2012 Highgate Society

Series Editor: Richard Webber

Publisher: Northern Heights Publications, 10a South Grove, London, N6 6BS

Distributor: www.northernheights.eu

Designer: Nicholas Moll Design

Printer: Rainbow Print Wales

A CIP catalogue record for this book is available from the British Library.

ISBN: 978-0-9572079-5-0

The Highgate Society

The Highgate Society was founded in 1966 to organise resistance to proposals to turn Highgate High Street into a lorry route. Today it has 1,400 members.

Thanks to the dedication and professional expertise of its members, the Society has gained an enviable reputation over the last 50 years for making Highgate a better place in which to live and work. Highgate is one of London's finest conservation areas and the Society protects its unique character by:

- Lobbying central and local government on matters of planning policy

- Working with residents, developers and planning departments to ensure high standards of development

- Campaigning for better public transport

- Playing an active role on consultative groups advising on the management of local open spaces

The Society sponsors a range of social and community activities, including an annual summer fair, winter carols and programmes of summer walks and winter talks.

The Society reports its activities through its quarterly magazine Buzz and regular e-mail bulletins. Its headquarters in Pond Square is open for coffee every Saturday morning from 10.30 to 12 and provides an informal planning surgery.

New members are welcomed and those with special interests and skills are encouraged to participate in the work of our Environment Committee and in our social activities. For more information, contact The Society at 10a South Grove, Highgate N6 6BS, or see **www.highgatesociety.com**

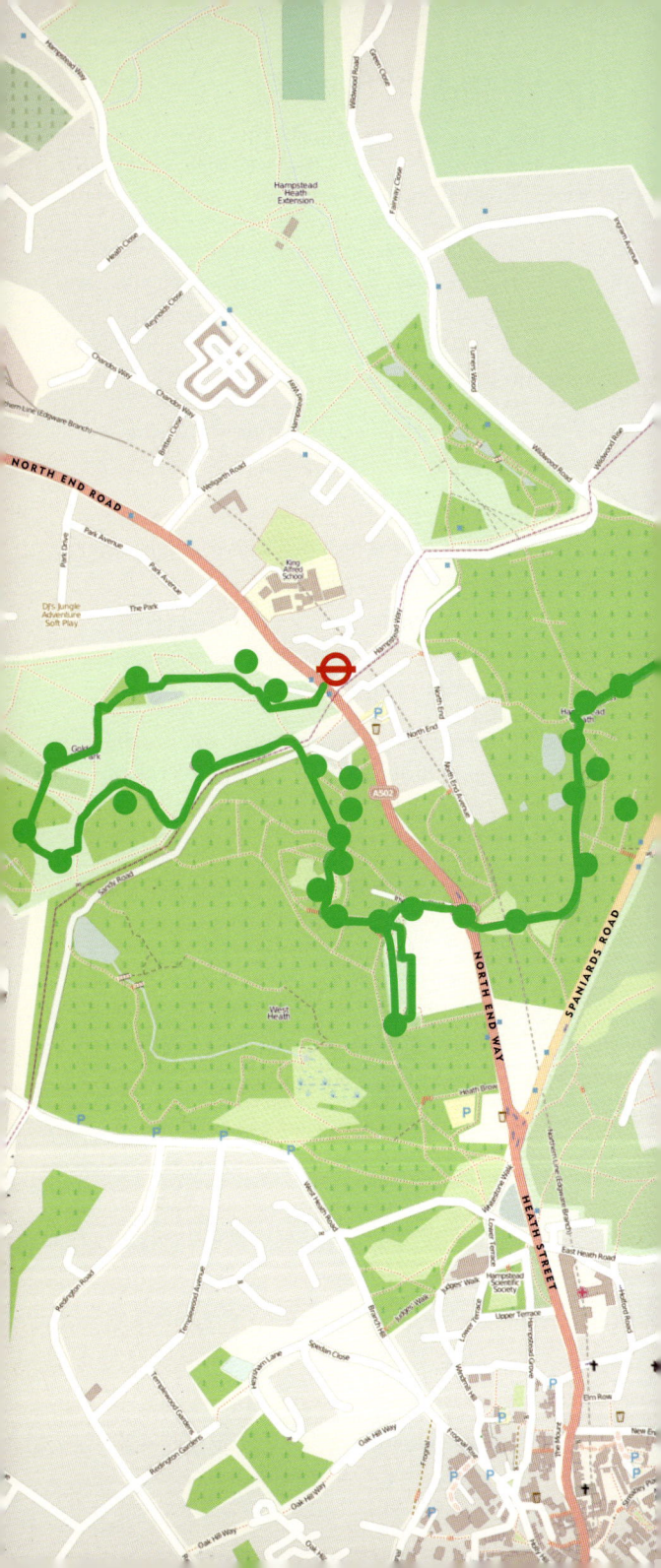